CONTENTS

Foreword

I. The Pairs
II. Heedfulness
III. The Mind
IV. Flowers
V. Fools
VI. The Wise
VII. The Arahat—The Worthy
VIII. The Thousands
IX. Evil
X. Punishment

XI. Old Age
XII. The Self
XIII. The World
XIV. The Awakened One
XV. Happiness
XVI. Affections
XVII. Anger
XVIII. Impurity
XIX. The Just
XX. The Path
XXI. Divers Verses
XXII. The Evil Way
XXIII. The Elephant
XXIV. Craving
XXV. The Mendicant
XXVI. The Brahmana

FOREWORD

The Dhammapada, of which a metrical translation by Mr. Woodward is here presented, is a precious Buddhist Scripture which deserves to be widely known. The Theosophical Society is to be congratulated on securing so competent and sympathetic a translator and on publishing it in a popular form.

The *Dhammapada* is a part of the *Khuddaka Nikāya* of the Buddhistic Canon and consists of about 420 stanzas in the *sloka* metre. Every fully ordained *bhikkhu*[1] is expected to know the book by heart, and its verses are often on the lips of pious laymen. The beginner of Buddhist studies can have no better introduction to Buddhism and must go back to it again and again to enter into the spirit of Buddha and his apostles.

The Scriptures of the Buddhist Canon are known collectively as the *Ti-piṭaka* (Sansk. *Tri-piṭaka*), "the Three Baskets or Treasuries". These divisions correspond to the two Testaments of the Christian Bible and contain (excluding repetitions) more than twice as much matter. They are known separately as the *Vinaya piṭaka*, *Sutta piṭaka* and *Abhidhamma piṭaka*, the Basket of Discipline, the Basket of Discourses and the Basket of Metaphysics. These scriptures are regarded with the utmost veneration by Buddhists as containing the word of Buddha (*Buddha-vacanam*), and are reputed to have been recited at the first Council held, according to tradition, at Rājagaha immediately after Buddha's death *circa* 540 B.C.

It seems more probable that they grew up gradually and did not receive their final shape till about three centuries later, at the Council held under the auspices of the Emperor Asoka at Pāṭaliputra *circa* 247 B.C. The account given of the First Council in the closing chapter of the *Culla vagga* seems to indicate that the Basket of Metaphysics was then unknown or unrecognised, and that the scriptures were then a *Dvi-piṭaka* (Two Baskets) rather than a *Ti-piṭaka* (Three Baskets).

If the *Culla vagga* account is accepted, it would appear that at this Council, expressly held by the Emperor for the consecrative settlement of the holy texts, the five Nikāyas or divisions which constitute the second Basket formed the subject of discussion between the President Kassappa and Buddha's favourite pupil Ānanda. The *Dhammapada* is a book of the fifth Nikāya. The *Mahāvansa* (Ch. v, 68) carries it back a few years earlier than the Council, to the time of the Emperor's conversion to the Buddhist faith, for on that occasion his teacher, Nigrodha, is said to have explained to him the *Appamāda-vagga*, which is the second chapter of the work. It was therefore known in the middle or early part of the third century B.C.

It seems to be an Anthology, prepared for the use of the faithful, of verses believed to be the real words of Buddha, short improvisations in which he expressed striking thoughts and embellished his preaching. They were current among the early Buddhists, and have been culled from the other scriptures as of high ethical and spiritual value. The importance of the *Dhammapada* for a critical study of Buddhism is thus considerable.

For a thorough understanding of the work and of the orthodox Buddhist view of it, it should be studied with the valuable commentary of Buddhaghosa. Buddhism owes a profound debt to this great man, and has recognised it in the name by which he is known in the Buddhist world. Says the *Mahāvansa* (Ch. xxxvii, 174): "Because he was as profound in his eloquence (*ghosa*) as Buddha himself, they conferred on him the appellation of *Buddha-ghosa* (the Voice of Buddha), and throughout the world he became as renowned as Buddha." He was an Indian Brahmana and a great Vedic scholar and apostle. On his conversion to Buddhism he became a not less ardent champion of the new Faith. He came to Ceylon from the cradle of Buddhism, "the terrace of the great Bo-tree" in Buddha Gāya, in the beginning of the fifth century, *i.e.*, nearly a thousand years after Buddha's death. He came in search of the old commentaries on the Tripiṭakas. The commentaries had been brought to Ceylon by the Emperor Asoka's son, the apostle Mahinda, and by him translated into Sinhalese. They continued to be orally transmitted until reduced to writing, in the reign of the Ceylon king, Vaṭṭāgamini (88-76 B.C.), at a convocation of learned *bhikkhus* at the cave-temple of Alu Vihāre in the Matale district.

The original Pali version having perished in India, Buddhaghosa, during his residence in the Mahā-vihāre at Anuradhapura, re-translated it from Sinhalese to Pali. His version supplanted the Sinhalese (since lost) and is now the only record remaining of the ancient tradition. He also wrote elaborate commentaries (*Aṭṭha kathā*)[2] on almost every part of the Tri-piṭaka and composed the *Visuddhi magga*, an extensive and systematic treatise on Buddhist doctrine, a veritable cyclopædia of Buddhist theology. His writings are regarded as absolute authorities in the interpretation of the Buddhist scriptures, and he is regarded as the second founder of Buddhism in Ceylon. He is held in high reverence also in Burma as the founder of Buddhism in that country (450 of the Christian era), having taken the Buddhist scriptures there from Ceylon.

Buddhaghosa's commentary on the *Dhammapada* mentions the occasions on which, and the audiences to whom, most of the verses were addressed by Buddha when, as an itinerant preacher, he went with his followers through the land—mid-Ganges valley and sub-Himalayan tract in the modern provinces of Agra, Oude and Behar; his watchwords—not wealth, fame or dominion, but peace, happiness, deliverance from the burden of sorrow and death, and his message: "Open ye your ears, the deliverance from death is found."[3]

When he first attained enlightenment under the Bodhi-tree (at Buddha Gāya), a descendant of which still flourishes in Anuradhapura, the oldest historical tree in the world, Buddha is said to have broken out into a song of triumph which is included in the anthology of the *Dhammapada* (153-4) and has been spiritedly rendered by Mr. Woodward:

> Through many a round of birth and death I ran,
> Nor found the builder that I sought. Life's stream
> Is birth and death and birth with sorrow filled.
> Now house-holder, thou'rt seen! no more shalt build!
> Broken are all thy rafters, split thy beam!
> All that made up this mortal self is gone;
> Mind hath slain craving. I have crossed the stream!

The way that he claimed to have discovered is known as the Middle Way (*Majjhimā Paṭipadā*), equally removed from an ignoble life of pleasure and a gloomy life of mortification, and consists in a realisation of the Four Great Truths (*cattāri ariya saccāni*) of suffering, its origin, its end and the path thereto. All existence, he declares, is suffering, its origin is desire, its end is the extinction of desire, to be attained by the Eightfold Path (*aṭṭhangiko maggo*) of right belief, right resolve, right speech, right act, right occupation, right effort, right mindfulness, right concentration and tranquillity.[4] The exposition and illustration of the Truths and the Way fill numerous tomes of the Buddhist scriptures.

It is these ideals of self-control, self-culture and heroic endeavour, the graces of wisdom, purity and love, the eternal law of *Karma*, or causality and moral retribution—under which every deed, good or bad, comes back most to the doer and yields fruit, helping or marring his progress—that are enshrined in the *Dhammapada* in luminous, pithy verse which lingers in the memory as a fountain of noble inspiration. They are almost too ethereal for human nature's daily food, and it is granted to few to realise in actual life these counsels of perfection unaided.

Buddha failed to make allowance for the weakness of humanity. His stoic agnosticism and self-reliant courage ignored God, denied the soul, repudiated worship and prayer and made man the master of his fate. This line of thought was not new to India, however stamped with his own personality. But human needs and aspirations have asserted themselves, and Buddhism has been compelled to absorb elements of doctrine and practice which he condemned. This has happened, especially, in the countries where the doctrine of the Mahāyāna (the Great Vehicle) prevails.

In China, Amitābha (Boundless Light), of whom Gautama Buddha is held to be an incarnation, and Kwanyin the Goddess of mercy, have laid great hold on the affections of the Buddhist population. Kwanyin (Sansk. *Kanyā*, the Virgin) is the gracious *Sakti* (Cosmic Power) of the Hindus,

> Mother of millions of world-clusters,
> Yet Virgin by the Vedas called.

In Japan, Amitābha is the Eternal one who is the Light, the Way, and the Life, and took human form to open the door of salvation to all. Kwanyin shares with him the sovereignty of Heaven. In Tibet are worshipped these and other emanations of heavenly beings—Manju Sri, the personification of wisdom, Avalokitesvara, "the Lord who looketh down" on the world with mercy to help and protect, Vajrapāna, and others, with a host of minor deities.

In Ceylon, which claims to belong to the purer faith, Buddhism is interwoven with the worship of, the popular gods of the Hindus and with animism and demonology. Under Mahāyānist influence Buddha has become a God, greater than others, but worshipped less fervently, for (as Robert Knox[5] found during his twenty years' residence in the island in the seventeenth century) the popular mind looks to Buddha for the soul, to the gods for the things of this world. His own doctrine remains a dream of philosophers.

Fifty years ago Buddhism was at one of the lowest ebbs in its history in the Island. The arrival of Madame Blavatsky and Colonel Olcott, the founders of the Theosophical Society, and their zealous propaganda, materially helped the efforts of the saintly Sri Sumangala to stem the tide, and there arose a renaissance which has had far-reaching effects. Colonel Olcott by his speech and writings did much to remove the prevailing ignorance and indifference, and recalled Buddhists to a sense of the value of their Faith.[6] He laid the foundation of that educational activity which has filled many parts of the Island with Buddhist schools and colleges.

Mr. Woodward is one of the noble band of Theosophists who have carried on Colonel Olcott's mission in Ceylon, and is perhaps the greatest of them all. Not being a Theosophist or Buddhist, I can speak of him more freely. Self-sacrificing zeal and devotion are commonplace words to use of him. They are often said of men, good and zealous in their way, who have had the compensations of good incomes and creature comforts, congenial friends and efficient fellow-workers. Mr. Woodward (or, to call him by his Sanskrit name, *Vanapāla*) was little favoured in these respects. His was a life of ascetic simplicity and self-denial and strenuous well-doing. An English gentleman of the best type, he combined in a rare degree the culture of the West and Bast, combined also the active spirit of the West with the mysticism of the East. He belongs to the roll of the great apostles of Mahayānist Buddhism who carried its message and its culture over the mountains and deserts of Asia to the Pacific Ocean. The Mahinda College, Galle, of which he was the mainstay for nearly twenty years, is a shining memorial of him. But who can estimate the gracious influence of his personality? The memory of it will be a cherished possession to his friends, young and old, and an inspiration to them all, and their gratitude and good wishes follow him unstintingly to his Tasmanian home.

P. ARUNACHALAM

Ponklar, Colombo
October, 1921.

Glory to Him, the Blessed Saint, the All-Enlightened one.

The Buddha's Path of Virtue.

CHAPTER ONE.

THE PAIRS.

1.
All states arising have mind for their causing,
Mind for their master, of mind are the offspring.
He who with foul mind speaks or does action—
Him pain pursues as the wheel dogs the ox-hoof.

2.
All states arising have mind for their causing,
Mind for their master, of mind are the offspring.
He who with pure mind speaks or does action—
Him bliss pursues, to him clings like his shadow.

3.
"This man abused me: he beat me and conquered,
Conquered and plundered." Cherishing in such thoughts,
Never appeased is the hatred of such men.

4.
"This man abused me, he beat me and conquered,
Conquered and plundered." Not having such thoughts,

Quickly appeased is the hatred of such men.

5.
Never by hatred is hatred appeaséd
Nay! but by kindness; that's the old-time Norm.[1]

6.
Others don't grasp this—"We men are mortals".[2]
Men who can grasp this soon end their quarrels.

7.
Looking for fair sights, unchecked in his senses,
In food uncontrolled, slack, inert, without vigour,
Death overwhelms him, as winds uproot weak trees.

8.
He who lives sense-restrained, heedless of fair sights,
Who in food keeps the mean, is trusty and sturdy,
Death cannot shake him: winds cannot move mountains.

9-10.
Without doffing his faults who would don the monk's yellow,[3]

Void of truth and of training, deserves not the monk's robe.

If he doff all his faults and be versed in the virtues,
In the training and truth firm, he merits the monk's robe.

11-12.
In the false seeing truth, and in truth seeing falsehood,

Men touch not the truth, but are fed on illusion.
But in truth seeing truth and falsehood in

falsehood,

Men touch the truth ever, feeding on right thoughts.

13-14.
As the rain through the roof of a house that is ill-thatched,
Lust leaks through the mind not composed by the training:
As rain never leaks through the roof that is well-thatched,
So through the mind well-trained lust leaketh never.

15.
Here he grieves and grieves hereafter: doubly grieves the evil-doer,
Grieves and suffers anguish when he sees the foulness of his deeds.

16.
Happy here, he's happy after: doing good he's doubly glad:
Glad, exceeding happy, when he sees the pureness of his deeds.

17.
Here he suffers, suffers after: doubly suffer evil-doers:
Thoughts of ill-deeds torture, much more torture when they enter hell.[4]

18.
He rejoices here and after: doing good he's doubly glad:
Thoughts of good deeds comfort, much more comfort when they enter heaven.

19.
Though reciting many verses,[5] if they do not what they preach,
Sluggards, counting others' cattle, cannot share the Brotherhood.

20.
Practising the Norm he preaches, though he utter verses few,
Quit of anger, lust and folly, truly wise, with thoughts set free,
Caring nought for this or that world, he hath part in brotherhood.

---

[1] *Dhammo sanantano* (Skt. *sanātāna dharma*). *comm. porānako dhammo*, the doctrine of the early tradition.

[2] See "Psalms of the Brethren," p. 177, trans. Mrs. C.A. Rhys Davids.

> "People can really never understand
> That we are here but for a little spell."

'Others' means all except the wise.

[3] A play on words, *anikkasāvo* (one who has not removed the *āsava's*, taints of lust, anger, delusion) and *kāsāvam*, the yellow robe. See note to v.21 re the use of the word 'monk'

[4] 'hell': '*duggatiṁ*, 'the evil path or destiny', a purgatorial state of rebirth.

[5] Texts of the sacred books, learned by heart by the Brahmins.

CHAPTER TWO.

HEEDFULNESS.

21.
Heedfulness leads to the Deathless;[1] heedlessness leads unto Death!

Heedful men live on for ever; they who heed not are as dead.

22.
Knowing this full surely, wise men take delight in heedfulness;

Heedfully they range with joy the pastures[2] of the Worthy Ones.

23.
Meditative, persevering, ever with strong might endowed,

Wise men reach the Blissful Haven, reach Security Supreme.[3]

24.
Heedful men's good name increaseth, if they strive with mind subdued

Pure in deed, with thoughts well-guarded, well-controlled of lawful lives.

25.
Let the wise man, striving, heedful, well-controlled and temperate,

Make himself an island which the flood shall never sweep away.

26.
Heedlessness the foolish follow, men of small intelligence;

As the best of treasures wise men guard the prize of Heedfulness.

27.

to Passion's snares; widespread bliss.

Heedfulness, looks down upon plains.[4]

wide awake, outstrips the fools.

the gods;[5] ever blamed.

fear in Heedlessness, and small.

in Heedlessness, Nibbāna's shore.

Cleave not thou to Heedlessness, cleave not thou
Strenuous and meditative, wisdom winneth

28.
Lo! the sage that drives away the cloud of sloth by
Climbing up the heights of wisdom, sorrowless
All the miserable beings, as a hillman on the

29.
Strenuous amid the heedless, 'mid the sleepers
As a racer beats the weak jade, so the wise

30.
Maghavā by Heedfulness attained the kingship of
Heedfulness is praised for ever; Heedlessness is

31.
Monks[6] whom Heedfulness delighteth, seeing
As the fire blazeth onwards, burn their fetters great

32.
Monks whom Heedfulness delighteth, seeing fear
Cannot fall into destruction; they are near

[1] '*amata-padaṁ*, 'the immortal lot', or simply 'the Ambrosial (nibbaṇa): the word 'immortality' in Buddhism does not imply 'a deathless Ego'.

[2] 'the sphere or range, *gocara*'.

[3] *Nibbāna*.

[4] 'literally,' as one standing on a mountain looks down on those standing on the level'.

[5] *Maghavā*, a name of Indra, the "sky-god," Jupiter. Human beings by great *tapas*, will power exercised, can attain this office.

[6] *"Monks"* does not convey the real meaning of *bhikkhu*, a mendicant ascetic wearer of the yellow robe.

CHAPTER THREE.

THE MIND.

33.
The fugitive, flickering mind,
Hard to guard and hard to bind,
The wise men train as they choose,
As a fletcher fashions a shaft to his use.

34.
Like a fish flung out on the bank;
Drawn from its watery home in a tank,[1]
Flutters this fugitive mind
To leave the realm of Māra behind.[2]

35.
Impalpable, hard to seize,
Eagerly rushing wherever it please,
Good is the taming of mind;
A mind well-tamed is a treasure to find.

36.
Invisible, subtle indeed,
Eagerly rushing its passions to feed,
Let the wise man guard this mind;
A guarded mind is a treasure to find.

37.
Wandering, dwelling apart,
Bodiless there in the cave of the heart,[3]
They who subdue this mind
Leave all the fetters of Māra behind.

38.
If he know not the Doctrine Pure,
If he waver in faith and be not sure,
If his mind be not strong-willed,
The cup of his wisdom is never fulfilled.

39.
If his mind be free from desire,
If his thought be free from anger's fire,
If evil and good he forsake,
There is no fear in the man that's awake.

40.
"Body's a vessel of clay;
Mind must be made like a fort," if he say,
Let him give battle to Mara, arrayed
In the weapons of wisdom, unafraid
Let him conquer and guard him and passionless stay.

41.
Soon, ah! soon on the earth
Will this body lie, a thing of no worth,
Neglected, void of the six
Workings of sense, a mere bundle of sticks.

42.
Whatever the ill that a foe
Doth a foe, whatever the grudge he may owe.
Greater by far will he find
The ill that is done by an ill-trained mind.

43.
Nay, not a father or mother
Could do so much; not a kinsman or other;
Greater by far will he find
The good that is done by a well-trained mind.

---

[1] *The tank* is earthly existence. The watery home is the world of desires.

[2] *Māra*—death, the personification of evil, rules the six highest desire-heaven-worlds: other great Gods are *Mahābrahma* and *Sakka* (Indra). *Yama* also, death, is the lord of the under-world. We may compare the Greek Gods, Zeus, Poseidon, and Pluto, who divide the rule of the manifested universe.

[3] Cp. v. 374, *suññāgāra*.

CHAPTER FOUR.

FLOWERS.

44.
Who shall discern this earth aright
And the Realm of Death and the World of Light?
Who shall choose out the Way
Of righteousness well displayed,
As a skilled hand chooseth a flower gay?

45.
The disciple[1] discerneth this earth aright

And the Realm of Death and the World of Light;
The disciple chooseth the Way
Of Righteousness well displayed,
As a skilled hand chooseth a flower gay.

46.
Seeing this body as like unto foam,
Illusive, by insight of wisdom alone,
Scattering Death's flower-tipp'd shafts,
He shall pass to a realm where Death is unknown.

47.
Culling life's blossoms here and there,
With his mind entangled by pleasures' delay,
Death comes and carries him off,
As a flood sweeps a slumbering village away.

48.
Culling life's blossoms here and there,
With his mind entangled by pleasures' delay,
Insatiate in desire,
Death makes him his bondsman and takes him away.

49.
As a bee on the wing flits from flower to flower,
Not harming the scent or the blossom's hue,
And is gone taking only the taste,
Let the sage his way through the village pursue.

50.
Not with other men's faults and other men's failings,

Nor the things they have done, nor the things left undone,

Should the wise man be concerned;
Let him look to his own things done and undone.

51.
Fair is the flow'r with its hue and its colour;
But if it lack odour its beauty is hollow.
So fair are the words well-spoken,
But how empty the words which deeds do not follow.

52.
Fair is the flow'r with its hue and its colour;
But if it have odour its beauty's not hollow;
So fair are the words well-spoken;
Well-spoken indeed are the words which deeds follow.

53.
As one from a heap of gathered flowers
Makes many a garland, many a crown;
So by a mortal being
Many a seed of good may be sown.

54.
The odour of flowers cannot prevail
'Gainst the wind, nor of sandal and *tagara*[2] fair;
'Gainst the wind goes the odour of saints;
The odour of saints goeth everywhere.

55.
Sweet is the sandal and sweet is the *tagara*,
And sweet of the lily the odour faint;
But of all sweet-savoured things
Sweetest by far is the scent of the saint.

56.
How small a thing is the odour of wood
Of the sandal or jasmine! How poor is their scent!
Yet the odour of saints prevails

E'en 'mongst the gods, most excellent.

57.
Men who live righteously, men who live heedfully,
Perfect in wisdom, rebirth have transcended:
Though he search for the prints of their feet,
Death cannot find them:[3] their journey is ended.

58-9.
On a heap of dung by the high road hurled,
As a lily may bloom and grow,
Delighting the mind with its fragrance pure:
So, lit by the wisdom of those who know,
'mid those who on the dung-hill grow[4]
A disciple shines out in the darkened world.

[1] "Disciple," *sekho,* one who has entered the Path, but has not become Arahat, who is *asekho,* Master.

[2] *Tagara*, an aromatic shrub.

[3] An Arahat at death leaves no *skandhas* or basis for another birth. Death, *Māra,* is pictured as hunting for a man's "rebirth consciousness". Cf. *The Book of the Kindred Sayings* p. 152 (Pali Text Translation Series).

[4] cf. Shakespeare, Henry V, I,1, 60.
　　'The strawberry grows underneath the nettle,
　　And wholesome berries thrive and ripen best,
　　Neighbour'd by fruit of baser quality'.

CHAPTER FIVE.

FOOLS.

60.
Long is the night to him that is waking,
Long is a league to the traveller worn,
Long is the coil of births
For fools that know not the truth of the Norm.

61.
If one find not a comrade to join him in travel.
Either like unto self or better than self,
It is safer to push on alone;
What fellowship can there be with a fool?

62.
"I am father of sons! I am owner of wealth!"
Thinks the fool in his folly and thereat is troubled.
He himself is not owner of self;
Much less is he owner of sons and of wealth.

63.
Wise indeed is he that knoweth his folly;

Fool indeed is the fool that thinks himself wise.

64.
Tho' a fool in his folly sit all his life long
By the side of a wise man, he never gets wiser,
For he knows not the Norm and its worth,
As the spoon never knoweth the taste of the broth.

65.
But a wise man that sits by the wise but a minute,
Quickly learns of the Norm and its worth,
As the tongue quickly savours the taste of the broth.

66.
Fools fare up and down with themselves for their foe,
And work evil deeds whose fruit will be bitter;

67.
Ill-done is the deed that brings sorrow in doing,
Whose fruit they will meet with tears and annoy;

68.
Well done is the deed that brings pleasure in doing,
Whose fruit they will welcome with gladness and joy.

69.
"O! how sweet!" thinks the fool, ere his wicked deed ripens.
When his wicked deed ripens he knows what is sorrow.

70.
Tho' month after month with the blade of a sword-grass[1]

The fool eats his rice grain by grain,
Not one fourth of a quarter of good doth he gain
Such as those who are stablished in Dhamma obtain.

71.
Now an ill deed, like milk, doth not change into curds,
But it burneth the fool—a live coal 'neath the ashes.

72.
Since his knowledge is born to a fool all in vain,
His good luck is lost to him wholly;
On his own head it falls; he is crushed by his folly.

73-4.
If a fool long for credit that is not his due,
Chief seats in the monks' hall,[2] respect from the Order,
And worship from laymen desiring;
"Let the monks and the laymen my deeds hold in honour
And in all things obey me, whate'er I may will—"
If such be the thoughts of the fool,
His pride and his longing increase in him still.

75.
"Success here is one thing, Nibbāna another:"
When a monk, the Buddha's disciple, is sure
Of this truth, he delights not in honour, eschews
The ways of the world and lives a recluse.

---

[1] An ascetic way of eating, supposed to be meritorious.

[2] Cf. N.T. "chief seats in the synagogue."

CHAPTER SIX.

THE WISE.

76.
If thou see a man of wisdom,
   Like a guide to treasure-trove,
Pointing out thy faults and failings,
   Follow him; such company
Brings prosperity, not woe.

77.
He who gives advice and teaching,
   And restrains thy feet from wrong,
By the righteous is beloved,
   But the wicked love him not.

78.
Have no fellowship with evil;
   Make no friends among the vile;
Make the virtuous thy companions;
   Follow thou the Perfect Men.

79.
They who drink the Good Norm's nectar
   Live in bliss with tranquil mind;
In the Norm by saints expounded
   Wise men ever take delight.

80.
Irrigators guide the waters,
   Fletchers straighten out the shaft,

Carpenters unwarp the timber,
   But the wise subdue themselves.

81.
As the solid rock for ever
   Rests unshaken by the wind,
Wise men rest unwavering,
   Troubled not by praise or blame.

82.
As a deep clear pool of water
   Lies unruffled by the wind,
To the Good Norm listening
   Wise men reach tranquillity.

83.
When the good men go about,
   Sensual babble is not theirs;
They, when touched by pain or pleasure,
   Show a calm untroubled face.

84.
Not for self and not for others
   Do they long for sons or wealth,
Not for rule, nor by injustice
   Self-advancement to attain;
   Righteous, wise and just are they.

85.
Few are they among us mortals
   Who have reached the further shore
Over yonder. But we others
   On this side fare up and down.

86.
They who hold fast to the teaching
   Of the Norm expounded well

They shall reach the shore and pass
   The realm of Death so hard to cross.

87-8.
Giving up the state of darkness,
   Let the wise embrace the pure;
Giving up home for the homeless
   Loneliness, where joys are rare,
Let him long for bliss unbounded
   Casting all desire aside,
Owning naught, and, firm in wisdom,
   Cleanse his heart from passion's stain.

89.
They whose mind is rightly tempered
   In the Wisdom's seven ways,[1]
Who have left desire behind them,
   Void of clinging, they rejoicing
Passionless and all-resplendent,
   Even in this world are freed.[2]

---

[1] The seven limbs of the Bodhi are:—*Sati*, concentration; *Dhammavicaya*, examination of mental processes or of nature; *Viriya*, energy; *Pīti*, zest; *Passaddhi*, calmness; *Samādhi*, mental balance; *Upekhā*, equanimity.

[2] *Parinibbutā*, let free from rebirth by having attained the state of *Nibbāna*, "gone out."

CHAPTER SEVEN.

THE ARAHAT—THE WORTHY.

90.
He for whom life's journey's over, free from

sorrow, free from pain not again.

Who has all the knots unfastened, suffering knows not again.

91.
Household life for them no joys hath; striving and intent in mind

As the swan deserts the marshes, every home they leave behind.

92.
They who gather up no treasure, feeding on the food that's known,[1]

They who range in mind the Void, the unconditioned formless Space,

As the bird's path in the ether, so their ways are hard to trace.

93.
They whose taints are all evanished, independent of support,

They who range in mind the Void, the unconditioned, formless Space,

As the bird's path in the ether, so their tracks are hard to trace.

94.
He whose senses now are tranquil, like a horse by trainer tamed

(Pride struck off, the taints[2] evanished), to the very gods is famed.[3]

95.
Like the solid ground unshaken, like the threshold of a door,

Like a pool by mud unsullied, such a saint is born no more.

96.
Calm the mind of such a being, calm his thoughts and words and deeds,

Set free by the perfect knowledge, liberated from life's needs.

97.
Self-dependent, self-sufficing, knower of the Uncreate[4]

Who hath loosed the bonds of action, from the chain of births set free,

All desires are fallen from him, noblest of all beings he.

98.
In the village or the forest, on the water or the ground,

Where the worthy ones are dwelling, there the earth's delights are found.

99.
Ah! delightful are the forests! where the worldling finds no joy,

There the passionless find pleasure, whom the senses do not cloy.

---

[1] literally, 'whose food is thoroughly understood' (as to its properties, qualities and purpose).

[2] The taints, *āsava's*, are three:—*kama*, desire; *bhava*, love of life; *avijjā*, ignorance. A fourth, *ditthi*, the holding of heretical views, is sometimes added. The gods are supposed to be still bound by these, and to envy the emancipated man.

[3] 'famed', literally 'by the gods is envied'.

[4] *Akataññu*, knowing the Unborn, the Eternal, the state of '*Nibbāṇa*', as in v.3 83:, but possibly here the context requires 'ungrateful', *i.e.*, not bound by ties of gratitude to anybody.

CHAPTER EIGHT.

THE THOUSANDS.

100.
Tho' one's speech be a thousand words,
   Vain words all strung together,
Better a single phrase
   Which calms the one that hears.

101.
Tho' a song have a thousand words,
   Vain words all strung together,
Better a single verse
   Which calms the one that hears.

102.
Tho' one utter a hundred songs,
   Vain words all strung together,
Better one verse of the Norm
   Which brings peace to the hearer.

103.
Tho' one conquer a thousand times
   A thousand men in battle,
Who conquers self alone
   Is the best of conquerors.

104.
Tis better to conquer self
   Than all this multitude;
If one be self-subdued
   And ever self-controlled,

105.

Not the gods or demi-gods[1]
   Nor the Lord of the world below[2]
Nor the God Supreme[3] have power
   To undo his victory.

106.
Tho' one for a hundred years
   Month after month should pray
With a thousand offerings,
   Yet if for a moment's space
He worship the feet of one
   Whose self is self-subdued,
His worship is better far
   Than his age-long offerings.

107.
Tho' a hundred years in the woods
   One tend the sacred fire,[4]
Yet if for a moment's space
   He worship the feet of one
Whose self is self-subdued;
   Such worship is better far
   Than his age-long offerings

108.
Not all the sacrifice
   That is offered in all the world
For a year, with a view to gain,
   Is worth a single quarter
Of the worship that is paid
   To the upright holy man.

109.
Whoso hath reverence
   For those advanced in years,
Four blessings thrive for him,
   Life, beauty, bliss and strength.

110.
Tho' one live a hundred years,
   Immoral, uncontrolled,
'Tis better to live for a day,
   Moral and well controlled.

111.
Tho' one live a hundred years
   Foolish and uncontrolled,
'Tis better to live for a day
   Wisely and well controlled.

112.
Tho' one live a hundred years
   Listless and lacking zeal,
'Tis better to live for a day
   While striving manfully.

113.
Tho' one live a hundred years
   Blind to the rise and fall,[5]
'Tis better to live for a day
   Seeing the rise and fall.

114.
Tho' one live a hundred years
   And see not the Deathless State,[6]
'Tis better to live for a day
   And see the Deathless State.

115.
Tho' one live a hundred years
   And see not the Norm Supreme,
'Tis better to live for a day
   And see the Norm Supreme.

[1] *Gandhabbo*, Skt. *gandharva*, those who preside over music and attend on the Four Great Kings.

[2] *Māra*, the Pluto of the Greeks, or Death-Lord.

[3] *Brahmā*, the Supreme Personal God or Zeus of Buddhism.

[4] *Aggihutaṁ*, Skt. *agnihotra*.

[5] *Udaya-vyayaṁ*, the law of *anicca*, impermanence.

[6] *Amatapadaṁ*, "the eternal lot," *Nibbāṇa*: see n. to v. 21.

CHAPTER NINE.

EVIL.

116.
Haste to do good; thy thoughts from ill restrain;
Sloth in good deeds makes one for evil fain.

117.
If thou do ill, cease, and thy sin forgo;
Take not delight therein; ill deeds bring woe.

118.
If thou do good, thy life in good employ;
Take thou delight therein; good deeds bring joy.

119.
Sinners see bliss while their ill deeds are green;
When the sin ripens, sorrow then is seen.

120.
Good men see ill while their good deeds are green;
When the good ripens, happiness is seen.

121.
Think not of ill: "It cannot be my fate";
As drop by drop the water fills the pot,
So slowly good men good accumulate.

122.
Think not of good: "It cannot be my fate";
As drop by drop the water fills the pot,
So slowly bad men woes accumulate.

123.
Just as the lord of some rich caravan,
Whose guard is scanty, fears the highwayman;
As one who loves his life must poison shun,
Be wise and guard 'gainst evil deeds begun.

124.
Thou mayest poison handle if thy palm
Contain no wound; whole skin no poison fears;
There is no ill for him that doth no harm.

125.
Who on a harmless creature worketh pain,
In whom no fault, in whom no ill is found,
Upon that fool his evil deeds rebound
As fine dust cast i' the wind falls back again.

126.
Some men by birth a life on earth attain;
The wicked go to hell, the good to heaven;
But holy saints are never born again.

127.
Not in the air nor middle of the sea,
Nor entering a mountain cave to hide,
Nor anywhere on earth can'st thou abide
Where from thy ill deeds thou can'st set thee free.

128.
Not in the air nor middle of the sea,
Nor entering a mountain cave to hide,
Nor anywhere on earth can'st thou abide
Where death shall not pursue and conquer thee.

CHAPTER TEN.

PUNISHMENT.

129.
All beings fear the rod, all fear to die;
Regard them as thyself; strike not nor slay.

130.
All beings fear the rod; all love their life;
Regard them as thyself; strike not nor slay.

131.
Whoso treats pleasure-loving creatures ill,
When he seeks bliss for self he shall not find it.

132.
Whoso treats pleasure-loving creatures well,
When he seeks happiness for self shall find it.

133.
Use not harsh speech; when harshly spoken to
Men may retort; painful are quarrellings,
And punishment may follow thy harsh words.

134.
If thou can'st keep thy tongue from wagging oft,

Silent as some cracked gong, thou hast thereby
Nibbāna won; no brawling is in thee.

135.
As with a stick the herdsman drives his kine,
So death and age compel the lives of men.

136.
The fool in doing ill knows not his folly;
His own deeds, like a fire, the fool consume.

137.
He who offends the harmless innocent
Soon reaches one of these ten states of woe;

138.
Sharp pain, disease, or bodily decay,
Grievous disaster, or a mind distraught;

139.
Oppression by the king, or calumny,
Loss of relations, loss of all his wealth,

140.
His house burned by a thunderbolt or fire;
At death, poor fool, he finds rebirth in hell.

141.
Not nakedness, nor matted hair nor filth,
Not fasting long, nor lying on the ground,
Not dust and dirt, nor squatting on the heels.
Can cleanse the mortal that is full of doubt.

142.
But one that lives a calm and tranquil life,
Though gaily decked, if tamed, restrained, he live
Walking the holy path in righteousness,

Laying aside all harm to living things,
True mendicant, ascetic, Brāhmin he!

143.
Who in this world is so restrained by shame
That, like a thoroughbred flicked by the whip.
He can think lightly of the lash of blame?

144.
By faith and virtue, energy, and mind
In perfect balance, searching of the Norm,
Perfect in knowledge and good practices,
Perfect in concentration of your thoughts,
Ye shall strike off this multitude of woes.

145.
As cultivators guide the water-course,
As fletchers straighten out the arrow-shaft,
As carpenters warp timber to their needs,
So righteous men subdue and train themselves.

CHAPTER ELEVEN.

OLD AGE.

146.
Laugh ye, rejoice ye, when this world is burning?
O wrapped in darkness, will ye not seek light?

147.
Behold this body decked, a mass of sores,
Sickly and swayed by multitudinous thoughts.
Impermanent, unstable, uncomposed!

148.
Poor worn-out carcase, home of sicknesses,
Fragile, corrupting mass, mere life in death!

149.
What joy to look upon these bleached bones,
Like useless gourds in autumn thrown aside!—

150.
A township built of bones and plastered o'er
With flesh and blood, the home and dwelling-place
Of age and death, pride and hypocrisy!

151.
Just as a royal chariot gaily decked
Falls to decay, so grows this body old;
But Truth and Norm old age cannot assail,
The holy ones indeed know no decay.

152.
Just like an ox, the witless man grows old;
His flesh grows, but his wits do not increase.

153-4.
Thro' many a round of birth and death I ran,
Nor found the builder that I sought. Life's stream
Is birth and death and birth, with sorrow filled.
Now, housebuilder, thou'rt seen! No more shalt build!

Broken are all thy rafters, split thy beam!
All that made up this mortal self is gone;
Mind hath slain craving; I have crossed the stream!

[1]

155.
They who in youth have never trod the way
Of righteousness, nor garnered wisdom's store.

Like herons in a fishless pool decay.

156.
They who in youth have never trod the way
Of righteousness, nor garnered wisdom's store.
Like broken bows, lie weeping their lost day.

---

[1] The triumphant words of the Buddha, when at last He attained enlightenment, Nibbāna, beneath the Bo-tree.

CHAPTER TWELVE.

The Self.

157.
Hast thou regard for self? Then keep thyself well guarded.

Be wise and keep good watch for one of the three watches.[1]

158.
First ground thyself in fitness; next, another teach.
Thus shalt thou wisdom gain and suffer no reproach.

159.
First carry out thyself whate'er thou teachest others.

Self-tamed, thou'lt tame another; but self is hard to tame.

160.

Self is the lord of self; who else could be the lord?
By taming self one gains a lord most hard to gain.

161.
The evil done by self, self-born and self-begotten,
Crushes the senseless fool, as a bolt the jar of stone.[2]

162.
He who is choked by sins, as a creeper chokes a tree,
Doth to himself what e'en his foes would have him do.

163.
Easy is ill to do and harmful to oneself;
But what is good and wholesome, that is hard to do.

164.
Whose rejects the words of noble righteous saints
On his own head brings ruin by his perversity,
As bamboo trees put forth their fruit and die away.

165.
By self is evil done; by self is one defiled;
Ill deeds not done by self to self bring purity;
Each for himself is pure; each for himself impure;
Thou can'st not cleanse another man's impurity.

166.
Mind thy affairs, not others', however great they be;[3]
Right knowledge of one's own brings more prosperity.

[1] The night is divided into three watches of three hours each. Some regard this passage as referring to childhood, youth and age.

[2] This may be translated, "as a diamond crushes the stony gem".

[3] Cf. *Bhagavad Gītā*: "Better one's own *dharma*, however ill-performed, than others' *dharma*, well-performed tho' it be."

CHAPTER THIRTEEN.

THE WORLD.

> 167.
> Follow not the way unworthy;
>   Live not thou in slothfulness;
> Let not doctrines false allure thee;
>   Turn thy thoughts from worldliness.
>
> 168-9.
> Stand! Arise! Throw sloth away;
>   Follow the path of righteousness;
> Happy he who walks aright,
>   Here and in the world to come.
>
> 170.
> As a bubble on the water,
>   As a phantom of the sands,
> Him who thus the world despiseth,
>   Death the king[1] cannot behold.
>
> 171.
> Lo! this world in all its splendour,
>   Like a royal car adorned,
> Wherein many a fool is seated,[2]
>   Hath no power to bind the wise.

172.
He who formerly was slothful,
　　But is slothful now no more,
Lighteth up the world with splendour,
　　As the moon from clouds released.

173.
He who, having once done evil,
　　Covers up his ill with good,
Lighteth up the world with splendour,
　　As the moon from clouds released.

174.
All this world is wrapped in darkness;
　　Few be they that are not blind;
Like the birds that 'scape the fowler,
　　Few be they that go to heaven.

175.
Lo! the swans fly on the sun's path,[3]
　　Fly by magic through the air;
Wise men from the world departing
　　Conquer Death and all his hosts.

176.
He who by false words transgressing
　　Breaks one tittle of the Norm;[4]
He who future life renounceth
　　Every wicked deed will do.

177.
Those who covet reach not heaven;
　　Fools care not for charity;
He who charity approveth
　　Reacheth heavenly joy thereby.

178.

> Rule on earth and joy in heaven,
>   Sovreignty of all the worlds—
> These are all by him transcended
>   Who hath entered on the stream.[5]

---

[1] *Maccurāja.*

[2] Reading *nisīdanti* for *visīdanti* ("are immersed").

[3] *Hamsā adicca-pathe yanti.* In Hinduism the *paramahamsa*, "the swan," is the mystic name for the liberated being (Cf. *Bhagavad Gītā*) who goes to the sun (*āditya* Skt.), and is reborn no more; also in *Chāndogya Upanishad*, VIII, 7-5, we read: "When mind ceases to act, he attains the sun. That is the way to the region above. It is open to the learned, but closed to the ignorant." Those who are reborn are said to go on the path of the moon. In Buddhism, the *Arahants*, Saints, have the power (*iddhi*) of flying through the air even physically, by self-levitation. Cf. V. 91.

[4] Cf. N.T.: "For whosoever shall keep the whole Norm, and yet offend in one point, he is guilty of all."

[5] One who has "entered on the stream" is an Initiate, *Solāpanno*, and is saved, *i.e.*, after seven more births, he reaches the state of *Arahat* and *Nibbāna* and is free from birth.

CHAPTER FOURTEEN.

THE AWAKENED ONE.

> 179.
> The Awakened One, unconquered Conqueror,
> Whose conquest naught in this world can undo.
> Who ranges o'er His boundless sphere untraced.
> By what tracks can ye lead Him to rebirth?[1]

> 180.
> Free from the snares of passion's outspread net,
> The Awakened One, whom longing cannot draw,
> Who ranges o'er His boundless sphere untraced.

By what tracks can ye lead Him to rebirth?

181.
Those sages who, to meditation given,
Delight in freedom's bliss, with mind controlled,
Gods envy Them, Those All-Awakened Ones.[2]

182.
To gain a birth as man is hard indeed;
'Tis hard to get one's living in the world;
Hard is the hearing of the doctrine true;[3]
Hardest to be an All-Awakened One.

183.
"Refrain thyself from every evil deed;
Stablish thyself in good; cleanse thine own thoughts"—

This is the message of the Awakened Ones.

184.
Long-sufferance is the best austerity;
Nibbāna, say the Awakened Ones, is best.

185.
"Revile not, harm not, live by rule restrained;
Of food take little; sleep and sit alone;
In meditation keep thy thoughts controlled"—
This is the message of the Awakened Ones.

186.
"Lust is not sated, tho' it rain gold coins;
Brief is the pleasure, great the pains of lust"—
Whoso saith this and knows it, he is wise.

187.
He finds no pleasure e'en in heaven's delights;
He finds his joy in slaying all desire,

That follower of the All-Awakened Ones.

188.
To many a refuge frightened mortals flee,
Mountains and forests, groves and sacred trees;

189.
These are no refuge safe, no sure retreat,
By these we are not from all woe released.

190.
He who takes refuge in the Awakened One,
The Doctrine and the Brotherhood, beholds
By right insight the Fourfold Noble Truths,

191.
Sorrow and sorrow's cause and sorrow's ceasing,
The Noble Eightfold Path that leads thereto—

192.
This is the refuge safe, the sure retreat;
This only from our woes can us release.

193.
Hard is that one of noble birth to find;
Not born in every land is He; the race
Wherein that Sage is born is prosperous.[4]

194.
Blest is the rising of the Awakened Ones;
Blest is Their teaching of the Doctrine True;
Blest is the union of the Brotherhood;
And blest to dwell together in unity.

195.
The Awakened Ones and they that follow Them,
Worthy to be adored, have conquered all

The hosts of evil, crossed the flood of sorrow.

196.
Whoso shall worship Them, the worthy Ones,
In whom desires are quenched and fear allayed,
None can declare the merits of that man.

[1] *Padam*, "track, footstep," may here refer to the *khandhās*, basis, or occasions of rebirth, destroyed by Arahants, cf. vv. 92-3.

[2] These verses may refer to any man who is "awakened," who has found "*Nibbāna*."

[3] This might mean, "it is hard to get a hearing of it".

[4] All *Buddha's* must be born in India, the sacred land.

CHAPTER FIFTEEN.

Happiness.

[1]

197.
O happily we live
   Angerless amid the angry!
O happily we spend our days
   Amid the angry angerless!

198.
O happily we live
   In health amid the sickly ones!
O happily we spend our days
   Amid the sickly ones in health!

199.
O happily we live
   Free from greed amid the greedy!
O happily we spend our days
   Amid the greedy free from greed!

200.
O happily we live
   Who have not anything at all!
Like ever-radiant gods above,

Our food immortal joys shall be.

201.
Hate follows victory;
    Conquered ones sit sorrowing.
But the calm live blissfully,
    Renouncing conquest and defeat.

202.
There is no fire like lust;
    No sin brings such ill-luck[3] as hate;
No pains so great as body's pains;
    No bliss is like the perfect Calm.[4]

203.
Hunger's the greatest plague,
    Embodied life the greatest woe;
Whoso knows this in truth, can say:
    "Nibbāna is the Bliss Supreme."

204.
Health is the greatest gain;
    Contentment is the greatest wealth;
Best kinsman is the trusty friend;
    Nibbāna is the Bliss Supreme.

205.
Who tastes the savour sweet
    Of solitude, who drinks of calm,
Is free from terror, free from sin,
    Draining the nectar of the Norm.

206.
'Tis good to see the saints;
    To dwell with them is blessedness;
If he should never fools behold,
    A man could dwell in happiness.

207.
The company of fools
   Ne'er fails to bring distress.
To live with fools brings suffering,
   As living with an enemy,
But wise men's company brings bliss,
   As being with dear relatives.

208.
If one be good and wise,
   Well-versed in lore profound,
Long-suffering, dutiful, a saint,
   Righteous and wise; if such there be,
Follow his footsteps, as the moon
   Follows the path of the stars.

---

[1] This chapter applies especially to those who have retired from the world.

[3] Ill-luck, *kali*, the unlucky throw in playing dice.

[4] *Nibbāna*.

CHAPTER SIXTEEN.

AFFECTIONS.

209.
He who applies his mind unworthily,
   Neglecting discipline,
Forsakes the goal and clings to things beloved,
   Then envies those to meditation given.

210.
Join not thyself to things beloved or loathed.
   To lack dear company,
To be with those we loathe, brings misery.

211.
Seek not for love; things loved when lost bring woe;

   Both are impermanent.
They have no bonds who dwell indifferent.

212.
Sorrow and fear are born of things beloved.
   From things beloved set free,
How canst thou sorrow? fearful how canst be?

213.
From things held dear, sorrow and fear are born.
   Set free from things held dear,
How canst thou sorrow have? how canst have fear?

214.
Sorrow and fear are children born of pleasure.
   No longer pleasure's slave,
How canst thou sorrow, fear how canst thou have?

215.
Sorrow and fear are children of desire.
   From all desire set free,
How canst thou sorrow? fearful how canst be?

216.
Sorrow and fear are things of longing born.
   From longing if thou part,
Thou hast no fear nor sorrow in thine heart.

217.
Upright and Norm-abiding, speaking truth,
    Who minds his own affair,[1]
That is the man whom every one holds dear.

218.
In whom is longing for the Nameless[2] born,
    Whose mind It hath enthralled,
Whose thoughts no longer are by passion torn,
    That man "a Climber of the Stream" is called.[3]

219.
As when a dweller in some far-off land
    Safe home returns at last,
Kin, friends and lovers waiting to greet him stand;

220.
So, when a man on earth good deeds hath done,
    When he hath passed beyond,
All his good deeds like kin, await that one.

---

[1] *Attano kamma kubbānam*, as in v. 166. Attends to his own spiritual progress without dictating to others how they should forward their evolution.

[2] "The unborn, uncreate, undeclared" state of *Nibbāna*.

[3] *Uddhamsoto.* (Skt. *Urdhamsrotas*) a name for the *anāgāmin* "non-returner."

CHAPTER SEVENTEEN.

ANGER.

221.
Conquer anger, banish pride;
    Every fetter cast aside;[1]
Clinging not to Name and Form,[2]
    Him who calleth nought his own
Sorrow never shall betide.

222.
He who rising wrath restrains,
    As one checks a whirling team,
Him a driver true I deem;
    Others only hold the reins.

223.
Wrath with kindliness allay,
    To the stingy freely give;
Conquer lying words with truth;
    Evil deeds with good repay.

224.
Speak the truth nor vexed be;
    Give, however scantily.
Following these maxims three,
    Thou the blessed gods shalt see.

225.
Sages harm no living thing;
    Self-restraint accomplishing
Such men reach the Deathless Lot,[3]
    Where all sorrow is forgot.

226.
Ever watchful, night and day
    Learning wisdom never cease;
In the one who strives for Peace[4]
    All the cravings die away.[5]

227.
There is a saying, Atula,
    Of old, not of to-day:
"They blame the man who silent sits,
    Or whose tongue wags alway;
And blame the man who keeps the mean;
    None in the world is blameless seen."

228.
There never was, nor will be, sure,
    Nor lives now among men,
A being blamed exclusively,
    Nor one entirely praised.

229-30.
But one whom men of wisdom praise,
    Watching him day by day,
Of faultless life, of holy ways,
    Thoughtful and wise, like Jambu gold,[6]
Who to blame such a saint is bold?
    Neither the gods, nor e'en Brahmā,
From him their praise withhold.

231.
'Gainst angry deeds be on thy guard;
    In body be composed;
All bodily misdeeds discard;
    With body tread the Way.

232. 'Gainst angry words be on thy guard;
    In speech be thou composed;
All wrongful ways of speech discard;
    In speech follow the Way.

233. 'Gainst angry thoughts be on thy guard;
    In thought be thou composed;
All wrongful ways of thought discard;

In thoughts follow the Way.

234.
In body sages are controlled;
　In thoughts as well as speech;
And they are Sages truly called
　Who are controlled in each.

---

[1] The Fetters, *saññojanāni*, are ten. These are cast off at different stages of the Path, until perfection is reached.

[2] *Nāma-rūpa*, "abstract and concrete," the five constituents of personality, *viz.*, mind and its factors with the four, body, feeling, perception, and mental functions.

[3] *Nibbāna*, 'the changeless, *accutaṁ*'.

[4] idem.

[5] idem.

[6] A precious gold from the Jambu river; others say, like rose apple in colour.

CHAPTER EIGHTEEN.

IMPURITY.

235.
Lo! Thou art now a pale and withered leaf;
　Death's messengers are close at hand;
Thou in the very gate of Death dost stand,
　And yet hast no provision for the way.

236.
Then make thyself an island of defence;
　Strive quick; be wise; when all the taints
Of dirt and dust are blown away, the saints

    Shall greet thee entering the Happy Land.

237.
Thy life has run its course; thou art come nigh
    The King of Death;[1] for thine abode
Thou hast no resting-place upon the road,
    And yet hast no provision for the way.

238.
Then make thyself an island of defence;
    Strive quick; be wise; blow off the dust
And stains of travel; wipe away the rust;
    So shalt thou see no more birth and decay.

239.
The wise and thoughtful man attacks his faults
    One after other, momently,
In order due, and rubs them all away,
    E'en as a smith blows off the silver's dross,

240.
Just as the iron rust accumulates
    Self born; and eats itself away;
So with the man who sinneth; day by day
    His own deeds to destruction lead him on,

241.
Texts not repeated oft are soon forgot;
    The house neglected soon decays;
Sloth is the bane of beauty; heedless ways
    Bring ruin unto him that keepeth watch.

242.
The taint of woman is impurity,
    And gifts by stinginess are spoiled,
And mortal man by oft transgression soiled
    Finds ruin here, loss in the life to come.

243.
Yet there's a taint far worse than any other.
   What is that taint? 'tis ignorance.[2]
Make yourselves free from this, O mendicants!
   Wipe off this stain and be ye undefiled.

244.
Life seems an easy thing to him that lives
   Wanton and shameless as a crow,
A fault-finder, who through this life doth go
   Immodest, insolent, and full of sins.

245.
But life's no easy thing for one restrained
   By shame, who seeks to walk aright,
All unattached, withdrawn from vulgar sight;
   Who liveth purely and hath eyes to see.

246-7.
He who takes life; whose mouth is full of lies;
   Who steals, and fouls another's wife;
A slave to drink, he even in this life
   The root of his own fortunes undermines.[3]

248.
O man I know this: "Not easy of control
   Are evil ways." Let not thy greed
And wickedness (of misery the seed)
   Become thy masters, lest thou suffer long.

249.
According to their trust and faith men give.
   Whoso regards with discontent
And jealousy the food for others meant
   Cannot get peace of mind by night or day.[4]

250.
But whoso disregards what others get,
　　Whose heart of jealousy is void,
In whom the root of envy is destroyed,
　　He gaineth peace of mind by night and day.

251.
There is no fire that burneth like desire;
　　No beast like hatred can devour;
No snare like folly to entrap hath power;
　　No river-flood can carry off like greed.

252.
'Tis easy to perceive another's faults;
　　Hard are one's own faults to descry;
A man will winnow others' faults like chaff;
　　But as the cheating gambler hides the die,
His own faults he conceals right carefully.

253.
Whoso is watchful for another's faults,
　　Testy and quick to take offence,
In him his passions will increase, and thence
　　Further is he from cleansing of his sins.

254.
The sky-path shows no tracks; no outward signs
　　The treader of the Path betray;[5]
The multitude in outward shows delay;
　　They who have won the Goal are free from all.

255.
The sky-path shows no tracks; no outward signs
　　The treader of the Path betray;
Nought lasts; all things embodied pass away;[7]
But nought can shake the All-Awakened Ones.

[1] *Yama*, Pluto.

[2] *Avijjā*, the first of the twelve links of the chain of causation and the last of the Fetters to be broken.

[3] Those are the five Precepts of Buddhism.

[4] *Bhikkhus*, mendicants, have to beg their daily meal.

[5] *Samano n'atthi bāhiro*. This verse is generally translated, "There is no true disciple outside the pale of Buddhism," and the commentary (P.T.S. text, vol. 3. p. 378) so translates these words, which the Buddha spoke to Subhadda just before His passing away. The context here seems to require the meaning "outward." Cf. v. 92 and vv. 179-80. The perfect leave no traces. "Sky-path," *ākāsa*, space.

[6] *Tathāgatā*. The epithet of the Buddha by which He usually describes Himself (cf. N.T. "He who was for to come"). See Sir (now Lord) Robert Chalmer's valuable pamphlet for the meaning of this much discussed epithet (J.R.A.S., Jan. 1898). *Nippapañcā Tathāgatā*, lit, "is free from the delays of human failings".

[7] *Saṁkārā*, all compounding factors of entities, persons.

CHAPTER NINETEEN.

THE JUST.

256.
He is not just who arbitrates by will.
He who by weighing right and wrong decides.
    He is a just man called.

257.
Not by his will, but with impartial mind
Keeping the Norm, thoughtful, who others guides,
    He is a just man called.

258.
One is not wise because his speech is long.
Long-suffering and harmless, free from fear,
    He is a wise man called.

259.
Not by much talk doth one uphold the Norm.
Who sees the Norm in action,[1] tho' he be
Of little learning, strenuous in the Norm,
   'Tis he upholds the Norm.

260.
Grey hairs do not a man an elder[2] make.
Tho' ripe in years, if all his age be vain,
   He may be dotard called.

261.
True, virtuous, harmless, moderate, restrained,
Wise and washed clean of all impurities,
   He is an elder called.

262.
Not by mere talk nor beauty of his form,
If he be grudging, greedy, fraudulent,
   Is any reverend called.

263.
In whom these faults are cut down, rooted out,
Who hath cast off his sins, who meditates,
   That man is reverend called.

264.
A shaven crown makes not the Samana.[3]
If such a one, lying and unrestrained,
Be full of lust and craving, how can he
   A Samana be called?

265.
But if he calm his faults, both great and small,
Since he all evil ways hath quieted,
   He is a Samana.

266.
He is no mendicant who begs his food.[4]
Not he who begs but he who keeps the Norm,
   He is a mendicant.

267.
He who hath good and evil laid aside,
Who wisely in this world walks righteously,
   He is a mendicant.

268.
He is no Muni who refrains from speech,[5]
If he be foolish and have wandering wits.
But he who holds the balance, grasps the real,
Who's wise to choose the good and leave the bad,
Who in this world sees both sides, is thereby
   A Muni truly called.

270.
He is no Worthy One who creatures harms.[6]
By harmlessness to every living thing
   A man is Worthy called.

271-2
Not by mere goodness nor by ceremonies,
Not by vast knowledge nor by ecstasy,
   Nor by a life retired,
Nor sleeping lonely, do I touch the Bliss
Of freedom which no worldly one can know.
By killing all desire, the mendicant[7]
Attaineth confidence.

---

[1] *Kāyena*, bodily action, may mean all the faculties combined.

[2] *Thero*, a "mendicant" of ten years standing in ordination is so called in the Buddhist "church".

[3] *Samana*, "ascetic," a title originally contemptuously applied to the Buddha and His disciples by the Brāhmaṇas. The word is etymologically derived from V. *sam*—to tame or quiet. Hence the reference in v. 265.

[4] *Bhikkhu*, "beggar," the name given by the Buddha to His ordained disciples.

[5] *Muni*, "sage, silent one." The Buddha was called Sakyamuni—"the sage of the Sakya clan."

[6] *Ariya*, "the noble, the worthy."

[7] Reading *vissāsam āpādi*. This verse is important as showing the Buddhist ideal in a nutshell. *Nibbāna* is the dying out of craving, the root of all evil.

CHAPTER TWENTY.

THE PATH.

273.
Best is the Eightfold Path: of truths, the four;[1]
    Dispassion in the best of states sublime.
Blest is he of human beings, who hath eyes to see.

274.
This is the way; no other way can lead ye
    To purify the mind and see the truth.
Walk this Way and free yourselves from Māra's host of ills.

275.
Tread ye this Path, and make an end of sorrow.
    Tread ye this Path for I myself have shown it.
Shown it after learning how to pluck away the thorns.[2]

276.
Strive ye yourselves; Buddha's but preach the way
    To them that strive. To meditation given

They who walk this Way are free from Māra's every bond.

277.
"All things compounded are impermanent";
    Whoso sees this with opened inner eye
Wearies soon of sorrow. 'Tis the Path of Purity.

278.
"All things compounded are of sorrow made";
    Whoso sees this with opened inner eye,
Wearies soon of sorrow. 'Tis the Path of Purity.

279.
"All states compounded are without a self";[3]
    Whoso sees this with opened inner eye,
Wearies soon of sorrow. 'Tis the Path of Purity.

280.
Whoso strives not when it is time to strive,
    Tho' young and strong, to sloth and folly prone,
Weak in will and thought, to knowledge never finds the way.

281.
Who guardeth speech and mind, who doth no wrong

    With body, making pure the triple way,[4]
He shall tread the Path of Wisdom by the sages shown.

282.
Wisdom is born of meditation deep,
    But lost by mind's distraction; knowing these
    Two paths of loss and gain, so let him live,
Let him so direct his life that wisdom may increase.

283.
Cut down trees and undergrowth, and from desire be free![5]

For from this jungle fear of danger's born;
Cut it down, O mendicants, and from desire be free!

284.
If but a trace there be, however small,
    Of lust of man for woman, as a calf
Clingeth to its dam, the mind in bondage will be held.

285.
Pluck out the love of self with thine own hand,
    Just as the hand an autumn lily plucks;
Tread the Way of Peace declared by Him who hath it trod.

286.
"Here in the rainy season will I dwell;
    And here in heat and cold." So thinks the fool,
Little recking of the dangers that may him befall.

287.
Care-stricken, with his thoughts of sons and flocks,
    Attached to life, Death comes and seizes him,
As a sleeping village by a flood is swept away.[6]

288.
Not all his sons have power to guard that man;
    No sire, no kinsman can protect him now;
How can kinsmen aught avail him in the grasp of Death?

289.

> The wise man, when he sees the truth of this,
> Restrained by righteous living in the Norm,
> Soon will clear the path that leadeth unto Perfect Bliss.

---

[1] *The Eightfold Path* is;—Right Views, Right Thought, Right Speech, Right Action, Right Living, Right Effort, Right Concentration, Right Mental Balance.

The *Four Noble Truths* are:—Ill, the cause of Ill, the ceasing of Ill, the Path.

[2] The *thorns* are the stings and torments of desire.

[3] These three *dicta* are the essence of the Buddha's teaching.

[4] The second, third and fourth steps of the Path.

[5] 'desire', *viz.*: '*nibbanā hotha*, 'be ye free from the jungle (or forest) of desire (*nir-vanā*, a pun on the word *nirvāṇa*), cf. v.344, *vanamutto*'.

[6] Cf. V. 47.

CHAPTER TWENTY ONE.

DIVERS VERSES.

290.
> If in giving up slight pleasure
>   Thou a greater bliss discern,
> Leave the lesser gain and wisely
>   To the greater profit turn.

291.
> He who causeth pain to others,
>   Seeking his own selfish bliss,
> By the bonds of hate encumbered
>   Hatred never can dismiss.

292. Those who disregard their duty,[1]
    Doing what should not be done,
Insolent and negligent in evil-doing
    More and more corrupt become.

293.
They who mounting guard on body,
    Ceaseless watch and ward preserve;
They who others' things neglecting,
    From their duty never swerve;
    They who, self-controlled, aspire,
    Concentrate in every nerve,
    Reach destruction of desire.

294.
Slaying father, slaying mother,
    With two kings of warrior fame,
And a realm with all its subjects,[2]
    Brāhmana's go free from blame.

295.
Slaying father, slaying mother,
    With two kings of saintly name,
And a fifth pre-eminent,[3]
    Brāhmana's go free from blame.

296.
They who, watchful night and day,
On the Buddha meditate,
    Are followers of Gotama.

297.
They who watchful night and day,
On the Dhamma meditate,

Are followers of Gotama.

298.
They who, watchful night and day,
On the Sangha meditate,
   Are followers of Gotama.

299.
They who, watchful night and day,
On the body meditate,
   Are followers of Gotama.

300.
They who, watchful night and day,
Take delight in harmlessness,
   Are followers of Gotama.

301.
They who, watchful night and day,
Take delight in ecstasy,
   Are followers of Gotama.

302.
O 'tis hard to give the world up,
   Yet the lonely life is hard;
Painful 'tis to dwell in houses
   With the uncongenial;
Painful travelling to and fro;
   Cease to be a traveller.[4]
Cease to be beset with pain!

303.
Faithful and of good repute,

Full of honour and renown,
He is reverenced and honoured,
   Whereso'er he choose to dwell.

304.
Holy saints are far-resplendent
   Like the peaks Himalayan;
Like the shaft that flies in darkness,
   Wicked men are never seen.

305.
Lonely sitting, lying lonely,
   Act alone and strenuous;
Taming self alone, rejoice thee
   In the ending of desire.

[1] *Kiccaṁ* "minding one's own business."

[2] The Brahmins used to claim that a "twice-born" saint was blameless, whatever his bodiless actions might be. The Buddha here speaks mystically. *Father* is ignorance, *Mother* is craving; the *two kings* are the great heresies of non-causation and nihilism. *The Kingdom and its subjects* are the six organs of sense (mind being the sixth); and the six objects of sense (form, sound, sight, smell, taste, thoughts), conquest of all these brings liberation from embodied existence.

[3] *veyyaggha-pañcamaṁ*, lit. 'a tiger-like man, as a fifth'. The Commentator explains this to mean the fifth of the Five Hindrances (lust, malice, sloth, pride, doubt) which beset the Path.

[4] *A traveller* is one who runs up and down the paths of rebirth.

CHAPTER TWENTY TWO.

THE EVIL WAY.

[1]

306.
The liar reaches hell, and he who says
   He did not what he did;
Both are the same hereafter, men of crooked ways.

307.
And many a one the yellow gown who wears,
   Wicked and uncontrolled,
By reason of his evil deeds in hell appears.

308.
Better for him who lives unworthily
   A red-hot ball to swallow,
Than eat the food the country gives in charity.

309.
Four states of ill to reckless men I tell
   Who seek the wives of others—
Ill-luck, a restless bed, an evil name and hell.

310.
Ill-luck, the Evil Way, short-lived delight
   Of fearful man with timid woman spent,
And from the king a grievous punishment—
   Let these four evils all adulterers affright.

311.
Just as a blade of grass not handled well
   Will cut the hand that grasps,
So doth the ascetic's life ill-handled lead to hell.

312.
Deeds done with sluggishness, the broken vow,
   The saintly life befouled—
Such evil deeds as these small recompense bestow.

313.
Act thou with energy, if act thou must:
   The careless mendicant
Doth but stir up a denser cloud of passion's dust.

314.
Leave evil deeds which afterwards bring pain;
   Better to do the good;
For when 'tis done that deed no sorrow brings again.

315.
Just as a frontier town that's guarded well,
   Which ramparts well defend on every side,
   So guard thyself, let not a moment slide;
Time-wasters suffer sorrow when consigned to hell.

316.
They who feel shame, where shame there should

be none,
>Shameless, where shame should be,
>Embracing doctrines false, down the Ill Path have gone.

317.
They who feel fear, where fear there should be none,
>Fearless, when they should fear,
>Embracing doctrines false, down the Ill Path have gone.

318.
They who see sin, where sin there can be none,
>Who see no harm in sin,
>Embracing doctrines false, down the Ill Path have gone.

319. They who know sin as sin, and right as right,
>Embracing doctrines true,
>Those beings enter on the Path of True Delight.

---

[1] *Niraya*, the Evil Path, the downward course to destruction, *duggati*, as opposed to *su-gati* the happy way or state of heaven.

CHAPTER TWENTY THREE.

THE ELEPHANT.

320.
As an elephant in battle bears the arrows at him hurled,

I must bear men's bitter tongues, for very evil is the world.

321.
Tamed, they lead him into battle; tamed, the king his back ascends;
Tamed is he the best of beings, whom no bitter speech offends.

322.
Good are well-tamed mules, and good are Scindian steeds of lineage famed;
Good indeed the mighty tusker; best of all the man self-tamed.

323.
Yet such mounts can nought avail us, cannot be Nibbāna's guide;
We can only reach The Pathless[1] on the self-tamed self astride.

324.
With the must from temples streaming, mighty Dhanapālako[2]
Captive, tastes no food, but longeth to the Nāga-grove to go.

325.
Sluggish, gluttonous and sleepy, wallowing idly to and fro,
Like a huge and grain-fed hog, a fool again to birth must go.

326.
Once this mind roamed as it listed, as it pleased a-wandering went.
As the holder of the *ankus* checks the furious

...elephant,

Now with wisdom I'll restrain it, guide it wholly to my bent.

327.
Take delight in earnestness; watch thy thoughts and never tire;
Lift thee from the Path of Evil, like the tusker sunk in mire.

328.
Hast thou found a fellow-traveller, upright, firm, intelligent?[3]
Leaving all thy cares behind thee, gladly walk with him intent.

329.
Hast thou found no fellow-traveller, upright, firm, intelligent?
As a king deserts his borders, by the enemy pursued,
Like the tusker in the forest, go thy way in solitude.

330.
Better is the lonely life, for fools companions cannot be;
Live alone and do no evil, live alone with scanty needs,
Lonely, as the mighty tusker in the forest lonely feeds.

331.
Sweet are friends when need ariseth, sweet is joy whate'er it be;
Sweet the blessing of life's ending, sweet to be from sorrow free.

332.
Sweet it is to be a mother, sweet the lot of fatherhood,
Sweet the life of holy hermits, sweet the life of Brāhmans good.

333.
Sweet is growing old in goodness, sweet is faith established,
Sweet to gain the prize of wisdom when desire for sin is dead.

---

[1] *Nibbāna*.

[2] A favourite beast of the king of Benares. The elephant, to the East, typifies wisdom, strength and endurance.

The Buddha is called *Mahā-nāga*, "mighty elephant"; The *nāga-grove* is *Nibbāna*. Those who wander in the jungle are those still bound by the fetters of rebirth.

[3] Cf. verse 61.

CHAPTER TWENTY FOUR.

CRAVING.

334.
Even as a creeper groweth,
　Creatures that are indolent
Find their craving ever grow;
　Like a monkey in the forest
Seeking fruit from bough to bough,
　So they wander to and fro.[1]

335.

He who yields to sordid craving
   That thro' all the world doth go,
Like the gadding vine that spreadeth,
   That man's sorrows ever grow.

336.

He who quiets sordid craving,
   Hard in this world to allay,
Like the dewdrop from the lotus,
   All his sorrows fall away.

337.

Lo! to all of ye assembled
   This the good advice I tell:
"Dig ye up the root of craving,
   As men dig the scented grass.
Let not Death so oft assail ye,
Even as the rushing torrent
   O'er the river reeds doth pass."

338.

If the root be still uninjured,
   Trees cut down will spring again;
If the root of craving liveth,
   Still there is rebirth of pain.

339.

When the six and thirty currents[2]
   Bring one under pleasure's sway,
Thoughts, like waves, with passion surging.
   Sweep him all confused away.

340.

Everywhere those streams are flowing;
   Now the creeper of desire

Plants its roots and standeth fast;
    Cut it ere it riseth higher,
Cut it with the axe of wisdom,
    Root the creeper up at last.

341.
Restless, wanton is men's craving;
    They who wander to and fro
In the restless search for pleasure
    Birth and death must undergo.

342.
They who in the trap of craving,
    Like a hare run to and fro,
By the fetters' bonds entangled,
    Long must sorrow undergo.

343.
Beings, in the trap of craving
    Like a hare run to and fro:
Mendicants who hope for freedom
    Must their passions all forego.

344.
Whoso, free from human passions,
    Junglewards to run is fain;[3]
Who, from lust emancipated,
    To his lust runs back again;
Lo! the man infatuated
    Plunges into bonds of pain.

345.
Not by ties of wood or iron
    Nor of rope (the wise men say)
Are men held in bondage strong;
But for jewels, wives and children,
They who passionately crave,

They are held in bondage long.

346.
But the downward-dragging chain,
   Yielding, hard to loose again—
This is bondage real (they say):
Who this chain of craving breaks,
   Free from lust, the world forsakes.

347.
They who yield to their desires
   Down the stream of craving swim;
As we see the spider run
   In the net himself hath spun.
Wise men cut the net and go
   Free from craving, free from woe.

348.
Loose all behind, between, before;[4]
   Cross thou unto the other shore;[5]
With thy mind on all sides free
   Birth and death no more shalt see.

349.
He whose mind is tossed with doubt,
   Seeing bliss in passion's surge,
Makes his craving grow the longer,
   Rivets all his bonds the stronger.

350.
He who joys in calming doubt,
   And the loathsome contemplates,[6]
Soon will Māra's bondage leave,
   Every fetter soon will cleave.

351.
He who hath attained the goal,

Fearless, free from lust and sin,
Who hath plucked out every thorn,[7]
Nevermore will be reborn.

352.
Free from lust, to nothing clinging,
   Who is skilful to interpret
All the wealth of sacred lore;
   All the mass of letters knowing
   (Whether after or before),[8]
This indeed is his last body,
He's a Master of The Wisdom,
Mighty Being,
   He indeed is born no more.

353.
Conqueror of all am I!
   Knowing all, from all conditions
Of existence I am free;
   By the slaying of desire
I have ended craving's fire.
Who could then my teacher be?
   I have now forsaken all,
I myself, by mine own knowledge.
   Whom should I my teacher call?[9]

354.
To give The Norm all gifts transcends;
   To taste The Norm is sweetest far;
No joy can with its joy compare;
   Who raving slays all sorrow ends.

355.
Wealth harms the fool; not him who runs
   To win the goal intent;
By lust of wealth the fool harms self
   With harm for others meant.

356.
Weeds are the ruin of the fields;
   This world by lust is spoiled;
Then great the fruit of gifts to those
   By lust who are not soiled.

357.
Weeds are the ruin of the fields;
   This world is spoiled by hate;
To those by hatred undefiled
   The fruit of gifts is great.

358.
Weeds are the ruin of the fields;
   Deluded are mankind;
Then great the fruit of gifts to those
   Whom folly doth not blind.

359.
Weeds are the ruin of the fields;
   Craving pollutes the world;
Then great the fruit of gifts to those
   By craving not enthralled.[10]

---

[1] In the round of rebirth.

[2] The six sense-organs and the six objects of sense (twelve) are affected by three desires of each, generally taken as *Kāmatanhā, Rūpatanhā, Arūpatanhā*, desire for existence in the world of desire, in the worlds of form, in the worlds of the formless (abstract), thus making thirty-six varieties.

[3] The jungle of passion.

[4] Past, present and future ties.

[5] Cross the stream to *Nibbāna*.

[6] One of the meditation exercises, to inspire loathing for the body and its corrupt nature.

[7] Cf. above v. 275.

[8] *Nirutti-pada-kovido*: skilled in the true meaning of the language (Pali) in which the Buddha taught.

[9] This was the reply of the Buddha to an ascetic who, struck by the Master's radiance after attaining *Nibbāna*, inquired who was His teacher and what was the cause of His joy.

[10] *Bhoga, rāga, dosa, moha, iccha*, riches, lust, hate, delusion, craving, are five of the hindrances to the saintly life.

CHAPTER TWENTY-FIVE.

THE MENDICANT.

360-1
Good is restraint of eye and ear, of nose and tongue,

 Of body, speech and mind; restraint is good
 In every way; the mendicant restrained
  All sorrow casts away.

362.
In hand and foot and speech whoso is self restrained;

 Whoso to ponder inwardly delights,
 Who liveth lonely and is well-content,
  Him men call mendicant.

363.
Whoso controls his lips, and words of wisdom speaks,

 Is not puffed up, who can elucidate
 The meaning and the essence of The Norm—
  Pleasant is he to hear.

364.
Who dwelleth in the Norm and in the Norm delights,

Who searcheth out and well remembers it—
From the True Norm that steadfast mendicant
   Will never fall away.

365.
Let him not think of little worth the alms he gains.
   Nor jealous be of alms to others given;
   For whoso envies other mendicants
     Wins not tranquillity.

366.
Though small the part of charity that falls to him,
   Whoso despiseth not the alms he gains,
   If he live clean, not given to slothfulness,
     E'en by the gods is praised.[1]

367.
Whoso hath neither part nor lot in Name and Form[2]

   (Who saith not "this is I" or "this is mine")
   And grieveth not for what existeth not,
     A mendicant is called.

368.
Whoso in friendly wise with all mankind abides,
   Firm in the teaching of the Awakened One;
   Reaches the bliss where all conditions cease,
     Reaches the State of Peace.

369.
O mendicants! bail out the water from this boat![3]
   Swift will it go when from this burden freed.
   Of passion and of hatred cut the root;
     Then shalt thou reach The Peace.

370.
Cut off the five; desert the five; the five subdue!

That mendicant, who from the fetters five[4]
Hath freed himself at last, by men is called
  "A crosser of the Stream".

371.
O mendicant! be meditative; let not sloth,[5]
  Let not thy passions toss thee to and fro;[6]
  Lest, swallowing the ball, thou burning cry,
    "Ah! this is suffering!"

372.
Who hath no wisdom cannot ecstasy attain;[7]
  Who knows not ecstasy, no wisdom gains;
  Whoso both ecstasy and wisdom hath,
    Unto The Peace is nigh.

373.
The mendicant, whose mind hath gained tranquillity,
  When he hath entered on his empty cell,[8]
  Hath joy beyond man's power to tell, for he
    The Truth discerneth well.

374.
Soon as he grasps the rise and fall of elements,[9]
  Such pleasure and delight thereby he wins
  As falls to them that rightly know the state
    Of immortality.[10]

375.
Let the wise mendicant in this world thus begin;
  Guard thou thy senses; next, with mind content,
  By discipline restrained, seek noble friends
    Who zealous live and pure;

376.

And by the laws of friendship act, live perfectly,
   And upright walk according to the Norm;
   Then in the fullness of thy joy thou shalt
     An end of suffering make.

377.

O mendicants! just as the snow-white *vassikâ*,
   The jasmine, putting forth fresh blooms to-day,
   Sheds down the withered blooms of yesterday,
     So shed ye lust and hate.

378.

Tranquil in body, speech and mind, O mendicants,
   Whoso in every way is well-restrained,
   Who all this world's desires hath thrown aside
     He is "the tranquil" called.

379.

Rouse thou the self by self, by self examine self;
   Thus guarded by the self, and with thy mind
   Intent and watchful, thus, O mendicant,
     Thou shall live happily.

380.

Yea! Self is guard of self and refuge takes in self;
   Just as a dealer trains a thoroughbred,
   A noble steed, and breaks him to the rein,
     So do thou self restrain.

381.

That mendicant, with utter joy and gladness filled,
   Firm in the teaching of the Awakened One,
   Reaches the bliss where all conditions cease,
     Reaches the State of Peace.

382.

Lo ye! a mendicant, though young he be, that

strives
>
> To grasp the teaching of the Awakened One,
> Lights up the world, as from a cloud released
> The moon lights up the night.

---

[1] Cf. vv. 229-30.

[2] *Nāma rūpa*, a traditional Vedic term for "mind and Matter," the immortal and the perishable, borrowed by the Buddha to stand for the mental and bodily compound in the individual, cf. *Buddhist Psychology*, Mrs. C.A. Rhys-Davids, pp. 23-5.

[3] The body with its needs and passions (water in the boat) hampers the progress across the stream.

[4]

> I. The first five fetters of *delusion of self, doubt, ceremonial observance, lust* and *ill-will*.
>
> II. The second five fetters of *desire for form, desire for the formless, pride, vanity* and *ignorance*.
>
> III. If the verb of the third clause, *vuttaribhāvaye*, be translated "pay attention to," as is possible, the meaning will be, "develop the five good qualities of *faith, zeal, concentration, meditation, wisdom*."
>
> IV. This may refer to the second five fetters, by throwing off which one becomes an Arahat.

[5] "Toss thee," reading *kāmaguṇā bhamiṁsu* (for *kāmaguṇe bhamassu*) as Prof. Dines Andersen suggests (p. 192, *Glossary to Dhammapada*. Pt. 2).

[6] Cf. v. 107. One of the tortures in the hells.

[7] "ecstasy," *jhāna*. There are four stages of mystic meditation leading to rebirth in the higher worlds.

[8] "Empty cell," *suññāgāram*, may refer to the meditation in the "cave of the heart," when all thought vibrations are stilled, cf. v. 37.

[9] "The rise and fall," reading *udayavyayam*. cf. v. 113.

[10] 'immortality': *viz.*: 'the Ambrosial'.

CHAPTER TWENTY-SIX.

THE BRAHMANA.

383.

Cut off the stream,[1] O Brāhmaṇa, right manfully;
   Repel desires; when thou hast known the end
     Of things conditioned, thou shalt be
       A knower of the Uncreate.[2]

384.

When by the twofold law (restraint and ecstasy),
   By virtue of the knowledge he hath gained,
     The Brāhmana hath crossed the stream;
       Then every fetter falls away.

385.

Whoso the stream hath crossed and from this shore hath passed,[3]

   Free from all cares, unfettered; one to whom
     This shore and that alike are naught;
       Him I deem a Brāhmaṇa.

386.

Whoso dwells meditiative, passionless,
   And free from all Taints, his course hath run,
     Whoso hath won the highest Goal—
       Him I deem a Brāmaṇa.

387.

"One who is rid of evil" is a Brāmaṇa;
   Samaṇa is one who tranquil hath become;
     "Gone forth from all impurity";
   The hermit is *pabbajjā* called.[4]

388.

Let not a Brāhmaṇa assail a Brāhmaṇa;
   Nor let him with the assailant angry be,
     Woe to the striker; greater woe

>>To him that, stricken, strikes again.

390.
No little profit cometh to the Brāhmaṇa
　Who hath his mind from pleasant things restrained;
　　Soon as the lust to harm is gone
　　　All sorrowing is laid to rest.

391.
Whoso offendeth not in thought and word and deed,
　In whom no evil from these three is seen;
　　Whoso is in these three controlled;
　　　Him I deem a Brāhmaṇa.

392.
If there be one from whom thou canst obtain the Norm
　Which He, the All-Awakened One, declared,
　　Revere him, as a Brāhmaṇa
　　　The sacrificial fire reveres.

393.
Not matted hair, nor caste, nor noble birth can make
　The Brāhmaṇa; but he that knows the truth
　　And knows the Norm, is blest indeed;
　　　And him I deem a Brāhmaṇa.

394.
Of what avail to thee, O fool, is matted hair?
　And what avails thy garment made of skins?
　　The outer part thou makest clean,
　　　But all is ravening within.[5]

395.

Whoso wears rags from dustheaps picked, whoso is lean,

With veins o'erspread, who in the jungle dwells
And meditates in loneliness;[6]
Him I deem a Brāhmaṇa.

396.
One is not Brāhmaṇa because of race or birth;
"Hail-fellow" is such called, and riches hath.[7]
Possessing naught, free from desire
Is one I call a Brāhmaṇa.

397.
Whoso hath cut all fetters off and hath no fear
Of what may him befall; whoso from bonds
And all attachments is released;
Is one I call a Brāhmaṇa.

398.
Whoso hath cut the strap, the leathern thong, the ropes[8]

And all thereto pertaining, and the bar
Hath lifted; him, the Awakened one;
Him I deem a Brāhmaṇa.

399.
He who endures, tho' innocent of all offence,
Abuse and blows and e'en imprisonment
With patience strong, a host in strength;
Him I deem a Brāhmaṇa.

400.
Who hath no anger, who to all his vows is true,
Upright in life, from passion free, subdued,
No more on earth to be reborn;
Him I deem a Brāhmaṇa.

401.
Who like a dew-drop on a lotus-lily leaf,
   Or seed of mustard on a needle's point,
      Clings not to any worldly bliss;
         Him I deem a Brāhmaṇa.

402.
Who knoweth even in this world his sorrow's end,
   Who bath laid down the burden of desire,
      Emancipated from his bonds;
         Him I deem a Brāhmaṇa.

403.
Whoso is deep in wisdom and intelligence,
   Who can with skill discern the right and wrong,
      Who hath attained the highest goal;
         Him I deem a Brāhmaṇa.

404.
Whoso with householders and wanderers alike
   Small dealings hath, who lives the homeless life,
      A mendicant of scanty needs;
         Him I deem a Brāhmaṇa.

405.
Whoso withholds the rod of painful punishment
   From living creatures, be they weak or strong,
      Who neither strikes nor makes to strike,
         Him I deem a Brāhmaṇa.

406.
Whoso forbearance hath to those that hinder him,
   And to the angry showeth gentleness,
      Among the greedy without greed;
         Him I deem a Brāhmaṇa.

407.

From whom all anger, hate, hypocrisy and pride
   Have fall'n away, as from a needle's point
     A grain of mustard-seed falls off;
       Him I deem a Brāhmaṇa.

408.
Gentle in ways and apt to teach his fellow-men,
   Whoso will utter truth and naught but truth,
     Whoso in speech offendeth not;
       Him I deem a Brāhmaṇa.

409.
He that takes nothing in this world that is not given,
   Whatever it may be, or great or small,
     Or long or short or good or bad;
       Him I deem a Brāhmaṇa.

410.
In whom is seen no more the longing of desire
   For this world or beyond, who hath no lust,
     Who hath no fetters any more;
       Him I deem a Brāhmaṇa.

411.
In whom is seen no craving, who, because he knows,
   Asks not in doubt the How or Why, for he
     Hath reached Nibbāna's peace profound;
       Him I deem a Brāhmaṇa.

412.
Whoso on earth hath passed beyond the opposites
   Of good and evil, and is free from grief,
     From passion and impurity;
       Him I deem a Brāhmaṇa.

413.
Who, like the moon on high, is stainless, pure and calm,
   Translucent and serene, who hath restrained
     The rise of all delightful states;
       Him I deem a Brāhmaṇa.

414.
Whoso hath trod the hard and muddy road of births,
   Hath crossed delusion, reached the other shore,
     Nor lusts, nor doubts, grasps not, is calm,
       Him I deem a Brāhmaṇa.

415.
Who homeless wanders through this world, a mendicant,
   Abandoning desires, who hath restrained
     The rise of sensual delight;
       Him I deem a Brāhmaṇa.

416.
Who homeless wanders through this world a mendicant,
   Abandoning his lust; who hath restrained
     The rise of craving and desire;
       Him I deem a Brāhmaṇa.

417.
Whoso hath left behind all ties that bind on earth,
   And e'en the heavenly world transcended hath;
     Whoso from every tie is free;
       Him I deem a Brāhmaṇa.

415.
Who joy and pain hath left, who from the heat of life

Is cooled, and hath no basis of rebirth,
    Heroic conqueror of the worlds;
        Him I deem a Brāhmaṇa.

419.
Who knows the rise and fall of things in birth and death,
    Who is not of the world, who hath the path
        Well trod, who hath become awake;
        Him I deem a Brāhmaṇa.

420.
Whose passage[9] hence the gods themselves cannot discern,
    Nor demi-gods nor men; a worthy one
        In whom the passions are subdued;
        Him I deem a Brāhmaṇa.

421.
To whom pertaineth naught of past or future things
    Or of the present; one who owneth naught,
        Who hath no wish for anything;
        Him I deem a Brāhmaṇa.

422.
Dauntless,[10] pre-eminent, heroic mighty seer,
    The conqueror, desireless one, made clean,[11]
        Whose eyes have opened to the light,[12]
        Him I deem a Brāhmaṇa.

423.
Who knows his former births, who sees both heaven and hell,[13]
    Who now at last hath reached the end of births;
        Perfect in knowledge he who hath done all things well,
        That sage I call a Brāhmaṇa.

www.ingramcontent.com/pod-product-compliance
Lightning Source LLC
Chambersburg PA
CBHW081625100526
44590CB00021B/3605